PRACTICAL WISDOM

PRACTICAL WISDOM

A Treasury of Aphorisms
and Reflections from the German

Edited and introduced by

Frederick Ungar

FREDERICK UNGAR PUBLISHING CO.

NEW YORK

Translations from the German by Sheema Z. Buehne, Alexander and Elizabeth Henderson, Edward Mornin, and Frederick Ungar

Copyright © 1977 by Frederick Ungar
Printed in the United States of America
Design by Anita Duncan

Library of Congress Cataloging in Publication Data

Main entry under title:

Practical wisdom.

1. Quotations, German.   I. Ungar, Frederick.
PN6092.P7   838'.02   76-15660
ISBN 0-8044-2932-4
ISBN 0-8044-6938-5 pbk.

For copyright acknowledgments, please see page 151

To my son Bertrand

Contents

Contents

What is the art of living? It is knowing how to subordinate the particular laws of one's life to the general laws of nature, the state, and society, and yet to preserve one's very self above all.

Arthur Schnitzler

Foreword

This collection of aphorisms and reflections takes its title from one major goal: to offer thoughts and perceptions of practical worth that can be of real help to people going about the daily business of living. These quotations direct us to writers from whose insights we may draw strength and courage in a period when it is all too easy to succumb to the materialism of a consumer-oriented society and the distracting influence of the mass media, and to despair over the perennial human condition. In such a time it may be useful to pause a while, and to turn to the words of thinkers and poets of past centuries and of our own— words that form a rich legacy of intellectual and spiritual attitudes. They can stimulate our thinking and enlarge our vision.

Here, then, are the words themselves, the words of great writers on matters of everyday life, religion and belief, education and self-realization, man and society, love and marriage, happiness and sorrow, freedom and oppression, peace and war, fate and chance, men and women, youth and old age. Significant statements on a wide range of subjects, professions of creed and ethical principles, formulations of political positions, and critical observations of educational and cultural value—all of them reflect the life experiences and philosophies of their authors and tell the reader what they have said or written on basic questions of human existence.

The touchstone for inclusion here was that the wisdom be practical, that is, based on experience that has potential for furthering life. Reflections equally profound or brilliant have been omitted because they did not serve the aims of this book.

On the ultimate meaning of life there is an overwhelming harmoniousness in the chorus of witnesses here assembled. Even when the thinkers quoted take opposing positions, as, for instance, in matters of religion, the reader will be challenged to clarify his own thoughts on the subject. He may be fortified in his present position, he may modify it, or he may take a great leap in a new direction. But he will not regret having faced the alternatives thoughtfully.

These aphorisms are characterized by incisive brevity and utmost clarity; the longer reflections come close to being brief essays. They constitute in a sense both a symposium of great minds and a means of aesthetic enjoyment. The reader will surely welcome the happy fact that truth and enlightenment are sometimes clothed in the pleasing apparel of wit or humor.

This volume is limited to the words of German writers and thinkers—for purely personal and pragmatic reasons. An autobiographical note may be in order. I spent the first forty years of my life in Austria, having been a publisher in Vienna before setting up as a New York publisher in 1940. In Austria, in my personal reading and as a publisher, I explored German literature extensively. My interest and familiarity with that literature have been maintained ever since.

I have also since assumed the task of publishing translations of worthwhile German books, making many available in English for the first time. Such "firsts" in English also apply to most of the quotations offered here, the work of several friendly translators. *German,* then, is to be read here as meaning "words offered by universal man that happen to be spoken in the German language." I have come to believe that today we are in greater need than ever of the words of the wise. That these words are pertinent to our time, I have no doubt.

It is my cherished hope that the purpose of this book will be achieved: to be a support to its readers in a difficult and troubling era.

Frederick Ungar

Authors Quoted in This Volume

7

God · Religion · Faith

Obscurantism and Rational Thought

Free Will and Fate

God · Religion · Faith

The idea of God is an absolutely necessary psychological function of an irrational nature, which has
nothing whatever to do with the question of God's
existence. The human intellect can never answer this
question, still less give proof of God. Moreover such
proof is superfluous, for the idea of an all-powerful
divine Being is present everywhere, unconsciously if
not consciously, because it is an archetype.

Jung

No one can know what the ultimate things are. We
must therefore take them as we experience them. And
if such experience helps to make life healthier, more
beautiful, more complete, and more satisfactory to
yourself and those you love, you may safely say: "This
was the grace of God." No transcendental truth is
thereby demonstrated, and we must confess in all
humility that religious experience is *extra ecclesiam*,
subjective, and liable to boundless error.

Jung

Religion is man's bond to God. It rests on reverential
awe before a supernatural power to which human life
is subject and which has in its control our weal and
woe. To put oneself in harmony with this power and
to keep it benevolent to oneself is the highest goal of
religious man and the object of his constant striving.

For only in this way can he feel safe from the dangers that threaten life, those that can be foreseen and those that cannot. Only in this way does he partake of the purest happiness, of the inner peace of mind which can be guaranteed by the firmest alliance with God and an unqualified, trustful confidence in his omnipotence and readiness to help.

Planck

"God" is a primordial experience, and from the remotest times humanity has taken inconceivable pains either to portray this baffling experience, to assimilate it by means of interpretation, speculation, and dogma, or else to deny it. And again and again it happens that one confuses God with one's own ideas and regards them as sacred. This is superstition and an idolatry every bit as bad as the Bolshevist delusion that God can be educated out of existence.

Jung

If I am asked whether it is my nature to render Him prayerful reverence, my answer is: Absolutely! I bow before Him as a divine manifestation of the highest principle of morality. If I am asked whether it is my nature to venerate the sun. I answer again: Absolutely! For it too is a manifestation of the highest, and is indeed the most powerful granted us children of the earth to perceive. In it I worship the light and the procreative power of God, through which solely we live and move and have our being, and all the plants and animals along with it. But if I am asked whether I am inclined to prostrate myself before a thumb bone of the Apostle Peter or Paul, then I say: Spare me and stay away with your absurdities.

Goethe

God · Religion · Faith

I honor religion—I know it is a staff to many who are weary, balm to many who languish. But can it, must it perform these services for all? Look at the world at large and you will see thousands whom it never so served and thousands whom it never will, whether they have been preached to or not.

Goethe

So long as every fool, every theologian, every rosary-sayer and every feuilletonist can make bold to evoke the word God to understand and to use as he finds convenient at the moment, every discussion on religious questions will remain unfruitful.

Schnitzler

He who believes in God may pray to him. He who knows God will make work his way of devotion.

Schnitzler

He who says there is a god says more than he knows, and so does he who says the opposite.

Kant

No man and no human institution may assert that it has more claim than any other to knowledge of God's truth.

Jaspers

That we divine God is only an insufficient proof for his existence. A stronger one is that we are capable of doubting him.

Schnitzler

Should I define what I understand by religiosity, then I would say: it is attentiveness and obedience: attentiveness to the world's inner changes, attentiveness to what is considered true and right; obedience that does not hesitate to adjust life and reality to this change, and so to do justice to the spirit.

Thomas Mann

Religious experience is absolute; it cannot be disputed. You can only say that you have never had such an experience, whereupon your opponent will reply: "Sorry, I have." And there your discussion will come to an end.

Jung

However profound and devout monism and pantheism may be, they do not lead us into the ultimate riddle of religion. It is the riddle of religion that we experience God in ourselves differently from when He confronts us in nature. In nature we comprehend Him only as impersonal creative power, but in ourselves as ethical personality.

Schweitzer

No matter what the world thinks about religious experience, the one who has it possesses a great treasure, a thing that has become for him a source of life, meaning, and beauty, and that has given a new splendor to the world and to mankind. He has *pistis* (faith) and peace. Where is the criterion by which you could say that such a life is not legitimate, that such an experience is not valid, and that such *pistis* is mere illusion? Is there, as a matter of fact, any better truth about ultimate things than the one that helps you to live?

Jung

The deeper our cognition of God penetrates, the further God recedes from us.

Ebner-Eschenbach

For reasons of morality it is necessary to assume the existence of God.

Kant

Things would be better in the world if every devout person did not think himself superior to the doubter in nobility of soul, nor every doubter to the devout person in intelligence. The doubter too can be a blockhead, the devout person a crook, and both can be both.

Schnitzler

There would be much less evil in the world if evil were not done in the name of God.

Ebner-Eschenbach

In their fight for the good, teachers of religion should have the inner greatness to abandon the doctrine of a personal god, that is, to forego that source of fear and hope out of which the priests of the past have derived such enormous power.

Einstein

Religion is the poetry of unpoetic men.

Grillparzer

There are also priests and bigots on the side of un-
belief.

Stoessl

I have been reading the Old Testament again. What a
great book it is! For me, what is even more remarkable
than the content is the way it is expressed, so that the
words seem like a product of nature, like a tree, a
flower, like the sea or the stars, like man himself. It
sprouts and flows and sparkles and smiles, one cannot
tell how or why, it just all seems quite natural. Truly
it is the word of God, whereas other books merely tes-
tify to the wit of man.

In Homer, that other great book, the words are
the result of art, and even if the matter, just as in the
Bible, is always taken from real life, it is nevertheless
given a poetic form, as though fused in the crucible of
man's intellect; it is refined by the intellectual process
we call art. But in the Bible there is not a trace of art.
The style is that of a notebook in which the pure
spirit, as though without any human aid, records the
day's events with much the same faithfulness to facts
as when a laundry list is made out.

There is only one writer in whose works I find
something that recalls the direct style of the Bible, and
that is Shakespeare. With him, too, the words sometimes have that terrible nakedness which terrifies and
overwhelms us. In his works we sometimes see the truth
incarnate, without any drapery of art. But that happens only in occasional passages where the genius of
art, conscious perhaps of its impotence, surrenders its
office to nature for a few moments, and afterward re-
asserts its authority all the more jealously in the vivid
characterization and in the ingenious elaboration of
the drama. Shakespeare is simultaneously both Jewish

and Greek, or rather the two elements, of the spirit and of art, have been reconciled in him, and by interpenetration have developed into a higher unity.

Görres

It is a plain, old book that looks as workaday and unassuming as the sun that warms us, as the bread that nourishes us; a book that looks at us with all the devotion and kindly blessing of an aged grandmother who with sweet, trembling lips and with spectacles perched on her nose never fails to read the book every day; and this book is called also quite simply the Book, the Bible. Rightfully, too, it is called the Holy Scripture. Whoever has lost his God can find Him again in this Book, and whoever has never known Him will feel emanating from it the breath of the Divine Word.

Heine

There is and always will be much controversy over the good or harm done by widespread Bible-reading. It seems clear to me that taken dogmatically and fancifully, it does much harm, as it has done hitherto; while taken didactically and feelingly, it is as useful as it has always been.

Goethe

Hence the Bible is an ever effective book; for as long as the world stands, none dare say: I comprehend it in whole and understand it in every detail. Let us modestly assert that it is awe-inspiring in the whole and applicable in part.

Goethe

Desperation is the only genuine atheism.

Jean Paul

Faith can mean nothing else but the conviction that life as such, with all its mysteries, all its horrors, and all its marvels, has a meaning. In any case, faith is a matter that has absolutely nothing to do with the mind; it is simply a matter of one's feelings, which, though related to character, must nevertheless be distinguished from it.

Schnitzler

There is only one true religion, but there are many kinds of creeds.

Kant

It is highly remarkable that forms of belief and superstition have remained the same for all peoples and in all ages.

Goethe

There are people who can believe anything they wish; they are happy creatures.

Lichtenberg

We must concede to everyone the right to believe what he has made himself believe rather than what others have made him believe.

Ebner-Eschenbach

For myself, the manifold facets of my nature make it impossible for me to be satisfied with but a single way of thinking. As a poet and artist I am a polytheist, while in my role as scientist I incline toward pantheism, and both tendencies are equally marked. When I stand in personal need of a deity, that also is readily provided for. The things of heaven and earth constitute so broad a realm that only the collective sense organs of all creatures are able to comprehend it.

Goethe

Knowledge and faith exist not to cancel but to complement each other.

Goethe

In truth, science and religion present no contrasts but rather for every person of serious bent they need each other for mutual supplementation. It is surely no accident that precisely the greatest thinkers of all times were also deeply religious, even if they did not care to exhibit in public what was most sacred to them. Only out of the concurrence of the powers of the mind and of the will has there evolved philosophy's ripest, most precious fruit: ethics.

Planck

Science can only state what is, not what should be. Outside its domain value judgments of every kind are indispensable. Religion, on the other hand, deals only with the evaluation of human thinking and doing; it has no right to speak of actual facts and the relations among them.

Einstein

Science without religion is lame; religion without science is blind.

Einstein

In matters of faith, whoever turns to reason gets un-Christian answers.

Busch

Belief and knowledge are like the two ends of a scale. To the extent that one rises, the other falls.

Schopenhauer

The unbeliever believes more than he thinks, the believer less than he thinks.

Grillparzer

Dogma is nothing else but the express prohibition of thinking.

Feuerbach

Religion restricts this play of choice and adaptation, since it imposes equally on everyone its own path to the acquisition of happiness and protection from suffering. Its technique consists in depressing the value of life and distorting the picture of the real world in a delusional manner—which presupposes an intimidation of the intelligence.

Freud

Religions are children of ignorance, which do not for long survive their mother.

Schopenhauer

It is those virtues that are praised most highly for which neither hard thinking nor much energy or self-conquest are required, foremost these two: patriotism and fear of God. Should there not be a justified suspicion that in themselves these are not virtues at all but are marked as such only by those authorities that derive the most obvious advantage from this view: state and church?

Schnitzler

If the believer finally finds himself obliged to speak of God's "inscrutable decrees," he is admitting that all that is left to him as a last possible consolation and source of pleasure in his suffering is an unconditional submission.

Freud

Even in being trainable man surpasses all animals. The Moslem is trained to pray five times a day with his face turned to Mecca and does so without fail. The Christian is trained to make the sign of the cross on certain occasions and to bow the head, etc. Altogether, religion is the masterpiece of training, that is, training of the faculty of thinking; hence, notoriously, one cannot begin too early. There is no absurdity, however manifest, that cannot be firmly implanted in people's heads, if only one begins to drum it in before the sixth birthday, continually repeating it with solemnity and gravity. As with animals, the training of men is fully successful only if carried out in early youth.

Schopenhauer

A touch of doubt makes faith nonsensical, cancels it out, as it were; while occasional fits of faith can hardly do any harm, they rather seem to confirm faith.

Schnitzler

The skeptic—the believer: should we not choose other designations for them, Instead of "the skeptic" would not "the inquirer" be better? (Because the skeptic is by no means unbelieving; he simply does not know what to believe. Since every religion has different articles of belief, all religions except one—and probably that one too—must be laboring under a delusion.) Instead of saying "the believer" it would be preferable to say "the credulous person"—to give it the kindest designation. Otherwise, "the superstitious person," "the lazy thinker," "the half-wit," or "the humbug." (The believer is arrogant in any case. He looks down upon the so-called skeptic with scorn, and indeed tends to hold him suspect.)

Schnitzler

Whether one makes an idol for oneself out of wood, stone, or metal, or puts it together out of abstract concepts—it remains idolatry, as soon as one has before oneself a personal entity to whom one offers sacrifices, whom one invokes, to whom one renders thanks.

Schopenhauer

Is it not strange that people are so fond of fighting for their religion and so reluctant to live in accordance with its commandments?

Lichtenberg

If you want to remove religion from our European culture, this can be achieved only by another system of doctrines, and this from the very beginning would take over all characteristic features of religion—the same rigidity, intolerance, the same prohibition against exercising thought in its defense.

Freud

To rob a man's life in this world in order to reward him in another means to cheat him out of his life.

Heine

That they preach in churches does not make lightning rods on their roofs unnecessary.

Lichtenberg

You learn of many a strict believer who has lost his faith in God because great misfortune befell him, even if it was his own fault; but you have not heard of anyone who has lost his faith because he met with some unmerited luck.

Schnitzler

Can there be anything more absurd than telling children, who have just only entered this world, things about another?

Kant

There is not sufficient love and goodness in the world to permit us to give some of it away to imaginary beings.

Nietzsche

If a god created this world, I would not want to be that god. Its misery would tear my heart apart.

Schopenhauer

As to blasphemy, nobody can prove that the blasphemed, the insulted, exists. Nor can one prove that, should he exist, he mandated anyone to stand up for him. Nor that, even if he had been insulted, he would not forgive. If blasphemy is to be forbidden on the grounds that the general public is offended, then one may say that the assumption of the existence of God has offended very many who are devoted to truth, and is still more offensive when such opinion is forced upon one and resistance calls forth punishment.

Freud

A healthy person needs neither immortality nor a god.

Schiller

Altogether, pantheism is nothing more than polite atheism.

Schopenhauer

Do I profess a religion? None, surely, of all you
    have mentioned.
Would you I tell you why? All for religion's sake.

Schiller

How trivial appears the belief that with the abandonment of religious ideas all poesy and heightened sentiment would disappear from the world. Quite the contrary! The world has become for me infinitely more beautiful and profound, life of greater worth and intensity, and death more earnest and thought-provoking, calling on me with might and main to fulfill my task and to cleanse my conscience, since I have no hope of making up in some other corner of the universe what I missed here.

Keller

There is no more beautiful worship of God than that which requires no image, and which springs from the dialogue with nature within ourselves.

Goethe

Man must cling to his faith that the incomprehensible is comprehensible, else he would cease to investigate.

Goethe

I am inclined more than many others to believe in a world other than the visible.

Goethe

Faith is love of the invisible, trust in the impossible, in the improbable.

Goethe

Who has art and science,
Has also religion.
Who does not have these two,
Needs have religion.

Goethe

That belief is the best through which man gains most and God loses most.

Hebbel

That religion is the best which unites the many, fortifies men, humbles the proud, and makes us love life and await death with acceptance.

Feuchtersleben

Everybody should put in order and satisfy his religious needs, and in this endeavor, enlightenment and education should be his helpers.

Keller

The highest happiness of man as a thinking being is to have probed what is knowable and quietly revere what is unknowable.

Goethe

Obscurantism and Rational Thought

Beware of engaging in discussion with people who are all too quick with pat counter-arguments from the fields of metaphysics and the unconscious. The cowardly fear straight thinking, and instead of making an honest fight with you in broad daylight, they prefer to slip away into the thickets of irresponsibility, and from an ambush they let fly poisoned arrows of phrase, paradox, and presumption, claiming that the obscurity they surround themselves with is inner illumination, if not divine inspiration from above.

Schnitzler

Admission to the field of metaphysical problems should be permitted only to those who have been found worthy by decent behavior within the realm of the generally accessible realities. To engage in occultism should be denied to everyone who is not sufficiently conversant with what lies within the relatively manifest; finally, no one who has not conscientiously paced off the regions of consciousness in all directions to the limits of luminousness, should be given the right to move in the regions of the unconsciousness. But it is naturally those realms of metaphysics, of occultism, and of the unconscious which are so difficult to check and which have such indefinite borders where adventurers, speculators, and imposters of thought feel most comfortable. And they may bring home the most chaotic reports from their excursions into those fields—there will never be a lack of fools or blockheads who will listen to them more credulously than to scientists whom profession, responsibility, and courage have qualified for their explorations.

Schnitzler

He was running a little business in obscurantism.

Lichtenberg

The further mankind's development progresses, the more it will be proven that we achieve true godliness not by anxiety toward life, fear of death, and blind belief but only by striving for rationality.

Einstein

Reason has been treated badly recently; it has been almost scorned by mystics, occultists, and the pious, because it has proved itself incapable of answering all that is asked of it. Has reason ever pretended to this? If it had done so, it would no longer have deserved to be called reason. Reason knows itself and knows its limits. It knows that it is no more than a small light in the dusk of eternity but in fact the only one at our disposal. It is true that it shines forth only onto the nearest surroundings; but should we put it out and walk fully in darkness if we do not belong to those who are satisfied with the uncertain flicker from above?

Schnitzler

Free Will and Fate

Can we really imagine a god who would simply be satisfied with creating the law of causality whereupon from the first impulse by which he set the world going, all subsequent events would spin off unalterably and predeterminately? No—he has not made it so easy for himself. He has set himself an equal adversary, free will, who is ready at every moment to take up the fight with causality and does so, even if he believes that he submits in humility to an inscrutable decree.

Schnitzler

The determinist puts the incomprehensible, the miracle, at the beginnings of all things. Is it less incomprehensible, less a miracle, less God than if he were always and everywhere at work? Would a god who after that colossal impulse let himself rest, disappear from the world, because everything now keeps moving by itself, in accordance with the law of causality, which he had created; would he not be equally miraculous as one who would have stayed, who would continue at work without let-up in every man, in every human thought, in every human stirring of will? And whither should that god of the determinists have disappeared? Whether he is now there or no longer there, he remains incomprehensible, remains a miracle, remains God.

Schnitzler

Without a belief in free will, our earth would not only be the scene of the most horrible senselessness but also the most unbearable boredom. Irresponsibiiity cancels out every ethical precept as soon as it enters consciousness. The self without a feeling of responsibility would no longer be the self, and the earth no scene of tragedies and comedies among individuals but a sad burlesque of free-wheeling drives, accidentally embodied in one individual or the other.

Schnitzler

Without the assumption of free will we would be forced to relinquish all our ethical concepts of guilt and atonement, benevolence and malevolence, meaningfulness and emptiness, and find designations for them that, without an attempt at aesthetic or moral evaluation, would give expression to the causal relationship alone. The idea of responsibility would be done away with: there would be no occasion to love or hate, to reward or punish, to admire or scorn, to pardon or avenge, to be proud or ashamed.

Thus it was not so much a moral and religious postulate to have free will enter as antagonist, which is, after all, nothing other than causality locked within the individual for the duration of his personal existence. It is rather an *aesthetic* postulate through whose fulfillment mankind succeeded in escaping from the deadly boredom of a world—without responsibility— which a strictly deterministic point of view had naturally to assume. According to this concept also, even the assumption of free will would have ensued only in accordance with the eternally operative law of causality, just as in the end also an idol would have to be looked upon not as an element opposed to the divine but as one element contingent upon the godhead.

Schnitzler

The fabric of this world is woven of necessity and chance; reason stands between the two and controls them. It takes necessity as the basis of existence and steers, guides, and uses what comes by chance.

Goethe

Anything that happens in the real world is determined and accidental at the same time; necessary in reference to its cause, accidental in reference to everything else.

Schopenhauer

Fate shuffles the cards and we play.

Schopenhauer

Don't even think of it. The future is an ingrate that torments the very people who most anxiously worry about it.

Nestroy

One builds true happiness for himself only by making himself independent of fate.

Humboldt

Certainly it is almost more important how man takes his fate than what it is.

Humboldt

I will put my hands into the maw of fate; it will never bow me down completely. Oh, if one could only live life a thousand times!

Beethoven

As if whipped on by invisible demons, the sun-steeds of time rush along with the fragile chariot of our destiny, and nothing remains for us but intrepidly to hold fast to the reins and to steer the wheels, now right, now left, here away from the rock, there away from the precipice. Whither the journey, who knows?

Goethe

All of us, as Schiller says, were born in Arcadia, that is to say, we came into the world full of claims to happiness and pleasure and cherish the foolish hope of having them fulfilled. But as a rule, fate soon comes along, takes rough hold of us and teaches us that nothing belongs to us but everything to it, that it has an uncontested right not only to all we own and earn, to wife and child, but even to our arms and legs, eyes and ears, and the nose in the middle of our faces. In any event, experience comes after a while to teach us that happiness and pleasure are a will o' the wisp visible only from a distance but vanishing when we approach; that on the other hand suffering and pain are real and anything but illusions. If the teaching is fruitful, we stop chasing after happiness and pleasure and concern ourselves instead with warding off suffering and pain as much as possible. When we realize that the best this world has to offer is a painless, tranquil, tolerable existence, we limit our claim to more in order to be surer of having our needs fulfilled. For the surest way of not being unhappy is not to demand to be very happy.

Schopenhauer

Youth and Old Age

Youth and Old Age

Everyone wants a long life, but nobody wants to get old.

Nestroy

One must grow old, that is, live long, to realize how short life is.

Schopenhauer

The first forty years of our life provide the text, the following thirty years its commentary, which teaches us fully to understand the true meaning and context of the text plus its moral and all its subtleties.

Schopenhauer

Age is a very courteous chap.
Knocks on the door with many a rap.
But bid him in no one does care.
And since he finds it cold out there,
At length he slips in quick and sure,
And now we call him a churlish boor.

Goethe

Why in old age do we see life, which we have behind us, as having been so short? Because we consider it as short as the recollection of it is. For from it has dropped everything insignificant and much that was unpleasant; little therefore has remained.

Schopenhauer

Our memory is like a sieve, the holes of which in time get larger and larger: the older we get, the quicker anything entrusted to it slips from the memory whereas what was fixed fast to it in early days is still there. The memory of an old man gets clearer and clearer the further it goes back and less clear the nearer it approaches the present time, so that his memory, like his eyes, becomes far-sighted.

Schopenhauer

As one on a ship recognizes that he is moving forward by objects on the shore moving backward, so does one become aware that he is getting older by the fact that even older people seem to be young.

Schopenhauer

In our youth, when we possess nothing, or at least do not appreciate quiet possession, we are democrats. But when in the course of a long life we have come to acquire property, we wish this not only to be secure but also that our children and grandchildren may have the undisturbed enjoyment of what we have acquired. Therefore in old age we are aristocrats, without exception, even if we leaned toward different sentiments in our youth.

Goethe

Youth and Old Age

When a man grows old, he should become mellow. I
see no wrong committed that I might not have committed myself.

Goethe

Error is all right so long as we are young, but we must
not drag it along into our old age.

Goethe

A human being would certainly not grow to be seventy
or eighty years old if this longevity had no meaning to
the species. The afternoon of human life must also have
a significance of its own and cannot be merely a pitiful
appendage to life's morning. The significance of the
morning undoubtedly lies in the development of the individual, our entrenchment in the outer world, the
propagation of our kind, and the care of our children.
This is the obvious purpose of nature. But when this
purpose has been attained—and more than attained—
shall the earning of money, the extension of conquests,
and the expansion of life go steadily on beyond the
bounds of all reason and sense? Whoever carries over
into the afternoon the law of the morning, or the
natural aim, must pay for it with damage to his soul,
just as surely as a growing youth who tries to carry
over his childish egoism into adult life must pay for
the mistake with social failure.

Jung

Aging people should know that their lives are not
mounting and expanding, but that an inexorable inner
process enforces the contraction of life. For a young
person it is almost a sin, or at least a danger, to be too

preoccupied with himself; but for the aging person it is a duty and a necessity to devote serious attention to himself. After having lavished its light upon the world, the sun withdraws its rays in order to illuminate itself. Instead of doing likewise, many old people prefer to be hypochondriacs, niggards, pedants, applauders of the past or else eternal adolescents—all lamentable substitutes for the illumination of the self, but inevitable consequences of the delusion that the second half of life must be governed by the principles of the first.

Jung

More even than that the happiness of our youth return, do we in old age long for the desires of our youth to return.

Ebner-Eschenbach

Man tends to forget his childhood as if it were an umbrella he left behind somewhere in the past.

Kästner

Whoever at a given age seeks to realize hopes and desires of his earlier years is doomed to deceive himself; for a man's every decade holds its own share of happiness, its own hopes and prospects. Woe unto the man whom delusion or circumstance persuades to reach forward or backward!

Goethe

In youth, everyone believes that the world began to exist only when he was born, and that everything really exists only for his sake.

Goethe

Young people would indeed be intolerable—but for the fact that I myself was once intolerable.

Goethe

An inexperienced youth thinks one can let old people go, because not much more can happen to them anyway: they have their lives behind them and are no better than petrified pillars of the past. But it is a great mistake to suppose that the meaning of life is exhausted with the period of youth and expansion; that, for example, a woman who has passed the menopause is "finished." The afternoon of life is just as full of meaning as the morning; only, its meaning and purpose are different.

Jung

I am finding that old age is not devoid of joys. Only hues and sources of these joys are different.

Humboldt

An old man forfeits one of the greatest rights; no longer is he judged by his peers.

Goethe

Nothing makes you age faster than the constant thought that you are growing old.

Lichtenberg

Do not resist the progressing years nor yield to them cowardly. Who does resist them will be dragged by the scruff. But who kindly meets them will be kindly led by the hand.

Speidel

One remains young as long as one can still learn, can still take on new habits, can bear contradiction.

Ebner-Eschenbach

I always distrusted old age very much and thought a decent person should betake himself out of life before he became a sorry copy of himself. And now I live to see, already a good way on the descending path, that I find life clearer, more tolerable than in my youth. Indeed I like it even better and will be very careful not to betake myself out of life, but would rather be a very merry old lady.

Kollwitz

The highest, the most varied, and the most lasting pleasures are intellectual, however much we may deceive ourselves about that in our youth.

Schopenhauer

Old age transfigures or ossifies.

Ebner-Eschenbach

We learn only in old age what happened to us in our youth.

Goethe

Youth and Old Age

He is the happiest who can integrate the end of his life with its beginnings.

Goethe

Aspects of Love

Aspects of Love

Eros is a questionable fellow and will always remain so, whatever the legislation of the future may have to say about it. He belongs on one side to man's primordial animal nature which will endure as long as man has an animal body. On the other side he is related to the highest forms of the spirit. But he only thrives when spirit and instinct are in right harmony. If one or the other aspect is lacking to him, the result is injury or at least a lopsidedness that may easily veer towards the pathological. Too much of the animal distorts the civilized man, too much civilization makes sick animals.

Jung

Anyone who overlooks the instincts will be ambuscaded by them.

Jung

Eros is a superhuman power which, like nature herself, allows itself to be conquered and exploited as though it were impotent. But triumph over nature is dearly paid for. Nature requires no explanations of principle, but asks only for tolerance and wise measure. "Eros is a mighty daemon," as the wise Diotima said to Socrates. We shall never get the better of him, or only to our own hurt. He is not the whole of our inward nature, though he is at least one of its essential aspects.

Jung

He does not love who does not see as virtues his beloved's faults.

Goethe

He to whom the object of his love is not at the same time his whole future, his conscience, and his eternal bliss, has never loved.

Nestroy

Confronted with great merits, there is no resistance but love.

Goethe

Voluntary dependence is the fairest state of all—and but for love, how would it be possible?

Goethe

Love is a nightingale, and it is peculiar to nightingales that in the dark foliage of the forbidden they sing much more enticingly than on the open flat road of duty.

Nestroy

Women always want to be our last love, and we their first.

Schnitzler

Where love reigns, there is no will to power; and where the will to power is paramount, love is lacking. The one is but the shadow of the other.

Jung

Aspects of Love

Love and necessity are still the best taskmasters.
Goethe

Their nerves of cobwebs, their hearts of wax, and their lovely heads of iron, this is the outline of the female structure.
Nestroy

With women everything is heart, even their heads.
Jean Paul

Women prattle too much when they get old; when they are young, they conceal too much.
Nestroy

In women, angel and devil get along better than anywhere else.
Börne

A woman never put to the test will always think too well of herself and too complacently of victory.
Jean Paul

When women speak about women, they always emphasize the beauty of the intelligent and the intelligence of the beautiful, that is, the peacock's song, and the nightingale's plumage.
Jean Paul

A girl who uncovers herself to her lover uncovers the secrecies of all womanhood; every girl is the guardian of female mysteries. There are places where peasant girls look like queens, and that goes for body and soul.

Lichtenberg

Nature destined woman to motherhood directly, to being wife only indirectly; conversely, nature made man more for a husband than a father.

Jean Paul

Every woman is more refined than her state of being. She gains more through education than men.

Jean Paul

In the eyes of a woman, he who flatters her is at first a rather clever man and soon thereafter quite an attractive fellow.

Jean Paul

Every woman considers her name passionately spoken the most beautiful, the most ingenious speech.

Nestroy

Love can occur in the twinkling of an eye, and even genuine affection must at some time have flamed up like lightning; but who will marry promptly when he is in love? Love is sometimes ideal, marrying sometimes real, and never is the ideal confused with the real with impunity. Such a fateful step must be con-

sidered from all angles and for a longer period of time
to find out whether all, or at least most, individual relations match.

Goethe

For young women nature has in mind what is called
dramaturgically a *coup de théâtre*. For a few years (at
the expense of the entire remainder of their lives) she
has endowed them with superabundant beauty and
charm, so that during those years they can take possession of a man's imagination to such an extent that he
is moved to the point of honorably assuming responsibility for their care as long as he lives. Pure rational
consideration alone does not seem sufficient justifica-
tion for such a step.

Schopenhauer

In our monogamic part of the world man loses
through marriage half of his freedom and doubles his
responsibilities.

Schopenhauer

Quarrels between married people are necessary, for
in this way they learn something about each other.

Goethe

It is a mistake for a taciturn, serious-minded woman to
marry a lighthearted man, but not for a serious-
minded man to marry a lighthearted woman.

Goethe

The bachelor has the misfortune of not having someone to tell him frankly about his faults, but the
married man enjoys this good fortune.

Jean Paul

The music at a marriage procession always reminds
me of the music of soldiers marching into battle.

Heine

A boorish man, however much he may be roasted on
the grill of love, will never turn into something agree-
able.

Nestroy

Verbal promises of marriage are in reality nothing
else but a somewhat more compact kind of lover's
oath; but for all that, they are still far from being a
serious matter.

Nestroy

Marriages are contracted in heaven; it is for that reason that this institution requires such heavenly patience.

Nestroy

One pays matrimony a very poor compliment by always calling "blessed" only the departed husbands
who have gotten over it.

Nestroy

If marriages can work toward peace, polygamy should
be allowed to the great.

Lichtenberg

A marriage without the spice of some dissension is almost something like a poem without an R.

Lichtenberg

He who is a best friend will probably also get the best wife, because good matrimony rests on the talent for friendship.

Nietzsche

Nobody should hope to get along with a wife with whom he quarreled when she was his bride.

Jean Paul

Marriage sets limitations for the individual, and thereby for the whole.

Hebbel

In my view, a single person's life is only a half one.

Mozart

Only man and woman together make the whole person.

Kant

This is still the only happiness in life: to love when two people respect and have tested one another.

Hölderlin

Marriage is the beginning and the peak of all cultivation. It makes the poor gentle and affords the most cultivated the best opportunity to show his gentleness. It must be indissoluble, for it makes for so much happiness that all individual unhappiness weighs as nothing in the balance. And why do they speak of unhappiness? It is impatience that assails man from time to time, and then he chooses to think himself unhappy. Let such a moment pass, and he will praise his good fortune that a relation of such long standing will still endure.

Goethe

It is hard to believe that this teeming world is too poor to provide an object for human love—it offers boundless opportunities to everyone. It is rather the inability to love which robs a person of these opportunities. The world is empty only to him who does not know how to direct his libido towards things and people, and to render them alive and beautiful. What compels us to create a substitute from within ourselves is not an external lack, but our own inability to include anything outside ourselves in our love. Certainly the difficulties and adversities of the struggle for existence may oppress us, yet even the worst conditions need not hinder love; on the contrary, they often spur us on to greater efforts.

Jung

Loving Kindness

Loving Kindness

Love him who is most remote from you as much as you cannot stand him who is closest to you, then someday perhaps there will be peace on earth.

Schnitzler

For every man with whom one comes in contact, one should not make an objective evaluation of his worth and importance but give an eye only to his suffering, his need, his anxiety, and his pains. Then one will always feel kinship with him, will sympathize with him, and feel compassion for him instead of hatred and contempt.

Schopenhauer

He practices the most forbearance who needs it least.

Ebner-Eschenbach

The people to whom we are support are those who are our support in life.

Ebner-Eschenbach

Ethics · Conscience · Truth

Ethics · Conscience

There are relative and absolute virtues. Relative virtues are those that can be regarded as expressions of a certain cultural epoch; absolute ones are those that will remain virtues at all times and under every circumstance; relative virtues: devoutness, physical courage, chastity; absolute virtues: truthfulness, intellectual courage, fidelity.

Schnitzler

Oh, learn to think with your heart and to feel with your mind!

Fontane

Only a life in the service of others is worth living.

Einstein

No aim is so high as to justify unworthy methods.

Einstein

Ethics is the science of the beautiful in us; aesthetics the science of the beautiful around us.

Coudenhove-Kalergi

What we call a bad conscience is always a good conscience. It is the good that rises in us and accuses us.

Fontane

Act as if the maxim from which you act were to become through your will a universal law of nature.

Kant

What you inflict on others, you inflict on yourself.

Lichtenberg

"Men's minds are trained largely at the expense of
their hearts." This is not so; it is only that there are
more educable minds than there are educable hearts.

Ebner-Eschenbach

I used to think that man must suffer to become strong.
But now I think he must have joy to become good.

Humboldt

Often we think we hate a person when actually we
hate only the idea that he embodies. And if that individual, who at a distance seemed intolerable or even
dangerous, confronts us in the flesh, we suddenly see
in him only a pitiful creature, condemned from birth
to sin, suffering, and death; and our hate is transformed
into empathy, compassion, perhaps even love.

Schnitzler

Forgiveness is the finding again of a lost possession—hatred an extended suicide.

Schiller

Just as torchlight and glare of fire look wan and insignificant compared with the sun, so are intellect and even genius, and likewise beauty, outshone and eclipsed by goodness of heart. The most limited intellect and ugliness, too, once they are accompanied by rare goodness of heart, are, as it were, transfigured by beauty of a higher kind, in that a wisdom speaks through them before which all others must fall silent.

Schopenhauer

Regard for the existence of human individuals, as the supreme human maxim, must govern all others, and this same regard must be the common bond that embraces all the peoples of the world.

Popper-Lynkeus

I am life that wants to live, in the midst of life that wants to live.

Schweitzer

Let me give you a definition of ethics: It is good to maintain life and to further life; it is bad to damage and destroy life. And this ethic, profound, universal, has the significance of a religion. It is religion.

Schweitzer

The heart always has a better conscience than the mind.

Stoessl

We don't remain good if we don't always strive to become better.

Keller

Our souls must change their linen every day if they are not to be wholly sullied.

Keller

There is one highest form of living, and this highest form is serving voluntarily.

Fontane

A new renaissance must come, one much greater than the renaissance with which we came out of the middle ages, the great renaissance in which mankind will discover that what is ethical is the highest truth and the greatest practicality, and that with it mankind will experience liberation from that miserable realism in which it just drags along.

Schweitzer

Truth

Nothing is great but the true, and the smallest aspect of the true is great. The other day I had a thought which made me put it like this: Even a harmful truth is useful, for it can be harmful only for the moment and will lead to other truths which always must become more and more useful. Conversely, even a useful untruth is harmful, for it can be useful only for the moment, leading us into other untruths which become more and more harmful.

Goethe

Truth is like a torch, but of gigantic proportions. That is why we hurry past it with dazzled eyes in fear of even getting scorched.

Goethe

Half truths are more pernicious than what is false.

Feuchtersleben

Lie knows more about truth than truth itself.

Stoessl

It requires a much higher sensitivity to seize upon truth than to defend error.

Goethe

A man's worth is measured not by the truth he may possess but by the sincere effort he made to get at the truth. For it is not the possession of truth but the search for it that enlarges his powers, and this alone brings him closer to perfection. Possession makes placid, idle, arrogant. If God held all truth in His right hand, and in His left hand the unique, eternally restless urge for truth, and, warning me that I was ever to err, He told me to choose—I would humbly deliver myself to His left hand and say: Father, give me that! Pure truth is for you alone!

Lessing

The purifying power of truth is so great that the mere striving for it spreads better air all around; the destructive power of the lie is so terrifying that the mere inclination to it darkens the atmosphere.

Schnitzler

You can lie to your conscience but you cannot deceive it.

Goethe

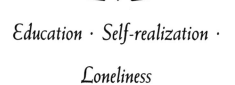

Education · Self-realization ·

Loneliness

Education

Education is the greatest task and the most difficult man can be charged with.

Kant

The best educational method is to give a child a good mother.

Lichtenberg

Educating mothers means training children in the womb.

Lichtenberg

The educator must hear childhood, not the child.

Goethe

What a child does should not be considered an action but a symptom.

Ebner-Eschenbach

A leaf that is destined to grow large is full of grooves and wrinkles before it develops. Now if one has no patience and wants it smooth like a willow leaf, there is trouble ahead.

Goethe

Beware of presenting a young person with the idea that success in its usual sense is the goal of life. A man is considered successful if he gets more from his fellow men than his services warrant. A man's worth should, however, lie in what he gives and not in what he can get.

Einstein

Who is educated only for his own time will turn out worse than that time.

Jean Paul

The most fruitful lesson is the conquest of one's own error. Whoever refuses to admit error may be a great scholar, but he is not a great learner. Whoever is ashamed of error will struggle against recognizing and admitting it, which means that he struggles against his greatest inner gain.

Goethe

Just because errors absorbed at an early age are usually ineradicable and the power of judgment is late in maturing, we ought to keep children up to their sixteenth year free from all theories which may contain great errors, that is to say, free from all philosophy, religions, and general notions of all kinds, and merely let them cultivate things in which error is either out of the question, such as mathematics, or at least not very dangerous, such as languages, natural science, history, etc.; but in general at any age only such subjects that are accessible and fully understandable to that age. . . . We should let the power of judgment, which presupposes maturity and experience, lie undisturbed and take care not to steal a march on it by the inculcation of prejudices, which will paralyze it permanently.

Schopenhauer

As we are constituted by nature, there is not a fault that could not turn into a virtue, not a virtue that could not turn into a fault.

Goethe

Children should be educated not for the present—that is done anyway—but for the future, nay, even for a more distant future. But one must know the spirit that one wants to flee.

Jean Paul

Woe to him who raises his child in fear, even if it is the fear of God.

Rathenau

Envy is aroused if a child is told to take the measure of his own worth by measuring himself in terms of others. He should rather judge himself by his reason. "Look how this and that child conducts himself!" An exhortation of this kind brings about a very ignoble way of thinking. If a person judges himself by the worth of others, he either tries to place himself above the other person or to reduce the other person's worth.

Kant

Who believes in the future, believes in youth. Who believes in youth, believes in education, believes in the meaningfulness and value of example.

Kästner

If we take people only as they are, we make them worse; if we treat them as though they were what they should be, we bring them whither they should be brought.

Goethe

It should always be the school's goal to release the young as harmonious personalities and not as specialists.

Einstein

Whoever knows only chemistry does not even know that properly.

Lichtenberg

The uneducated man sees everywhere only isolated objects, the half-educated the rule, the educated the exception.

Grillparzer

If people are taught how to think and not always what to think, a false concept will be guarded against.

Lichtenberg

Nothing will strengthen a man more than the confidence shown in him.

Goethe

Self-realization

————•———

We must *be* nothing but rather must will to *become* everything.

Schiller

Can man really be destined to neglect developing himself for any end whatever?

Schiller

I do believe that every individual human soul that develops its powers is more than the greatest society taken as a whole. The greatest state is a work of man; man is the work of incomparably great Nature. The state is a product of chance, but man is a necessary being, and by what is the state great and venerable except the power of its individuals? The state is only a product of human endeavor, it is a creation of thought, but man is himself the source of the endeavor and the creator of the thought.

Schiller

People speak of happiness and misfortune that heaven brings them. What people call happiness and misfortune is only the raw material for it. It is up to man what he makes of it. It is not heaven that brings happiness, it is man who makes his happiness in his own breast. Man should not worry that he get into heaven, but rather that heaven get into him. Who does not carry heaven within himself will seek heaven in vain in all the universe.

Ludwig

Nobody can contribute to the best of humanity who does not make the best out of himself.

Herder

Live with your century, but be not its creature.

Schiller

Loneliness

In loneliness, when everybody is thrown on his own resources, it becomes apparent what his inner resources are. Then the high-placed dunce sighs under the burden of his paltry individuality, while the highly gifted populates and enlivens the dreariest environment with his thoughts.

Schopenhauer

Each person can be wholly himself only as long as he is alone. He who does not love solitude, does not love freedom, for only he who is alone is free.

Schopenhauer

I cannot understand how certain people seek to lay claim to intellectual stature, nobility of soul, and strength of character, yet have not the slightest feeling for being alone, for solitude. I maintain that when joined with a quiet contemplation of nature, a serene and conscious faith in creation and the Creator is the only true school for a mind of fine potential.

Goethe

What makes people sociable is their inability to endure loneliness, and thus themselves.

Schopenhauer

I never feel less lonely than when I am alone.

Nestroy

Twice in one's life one must be lonely: in youth, to learn much and to acquire a way of thinking that will stand up through life; and again in old age, to ponder over everything we experienced, all the flowers we picked, and over all the storms of fate.

Immermann

Learning to endure loneliness should be a main study of young people because it is the source of happiness and peace of mind.

Schopenhauer

He who feels condemned to loneliness can still do much to make his loneliness blessed.

Schnitzler

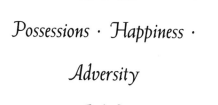

Possessions · *Happiness* ·

Adversity

Possessions

From time to time we should strive to look at our possessions as they would seem to us if we had lost them, and this applies to everything, to property, health, friends, loves, wife, child, horse, and dog. As a rule loss only teaches us the true value of everything.

Schopenhauer

We are not rich by what we possess but rather by what we can do without with dignity. Mankind may well become richer by becoming poorer and gain by losing.

Kant

Wealth is like sea water; the more we drink of it, the thirstier we become.

Schopenhauer

Property should be considered as a bulwark against the many ills and misfortunes, not as a license or even an obligation to procure the pleasures of the world.

Schopenhauer

If there is not always something dearer than life, then life is not worth much.

Seume

Ideas are indeed the only truly enduring things in life. Once one is used to living among ideas, sorrows and accidents lose their sting. One may be wistful and sad but never impatient or helpless.

Humboldt

If only the rich people would not invite again rich but poor people, then all people would have enough to eat.

Nestroy

What a man is in himself, what accompanies him when he is alone, what no one can give him or take away, is more essential to him than everything he has in the way of possessions, or even what he may be in the eyes of the world.

Schopenhauer

Poverty is no doubt the worst thing. If someone placed ten million before me saying I was to keep the money and accept poverty, I wouldn't take it.

Nestroy

Happiness

Happiness belongs to those who are sufficient unto themselves. For all external sources of happiness and pleasure are, by their very nature, highly uncertain, precarious, ephemeral, and subject to chance.

Schopenhauer

Happiness

No man's life, even the happiest, is without its struggles and sacrifices, for genuine happiness comes to each of us only insofar as our emotions make us independent of fate.

Humboldt

Man has no concern for the happiness or unhappiness of others as long as he himself is not contented. See to it then that he is content with little; then man will be kind-hearted.

Kant

In judging the happiness of one who is young, handsome, rich, and respected, the question must be asked whether he is, with all that, of cheerful temperament. For if he is of good cheer, it makes no difference whether he is young or old, straight or hunchbacked, rich or poor: he is happy.

Schopenhauer

This is certain that he alone is happy and great who has neither to rule nor to obey in order to be somebody.

Goethe

To say that very many people are unhappier than you does not provide a roof over one's head, but it is good enough to take cover during a shower.

Lichtenberg

Man is a god when he dreams, a beggar when he reasons.

Hölderlin

There is really no enjoyment other than in being aware of our powers and using them, and the greatest pain is to become aware of their lack when they are needed.

Schopenhauer

With a modicum of character man can conceal his unhappiness splendidly, but as to happiness . . . there every breath becomes a herald's trumpet, every motion shouts it from the rooftops: here can be seen a colossal bliss.

Nestroy

The main thing is that you hear life's music everywhere. Most people hear only its dissonances.

Fontane

Where a man stands inspired is the top of the world.

Eichendorff

To feel happy—even without happiness—that is happiness.

Ebner-Eschenbach

Adversity

———◆•◆———

Great necessity ennobles man, petty need humiliates him.

Goethe

Providence has a thousand means to raise the fallen and lift up the prostrate. Sometimes our fate resembles a fruit tree in winter. Who would think at beholding such a sad sight that those rigid branches, those jagged twigs will turn green again in the spring and blossom and bear fruit, but we hope it, we know it.

Goethe

Perhaps the greatest thing that can be said to a man's credit is that he gains the greatest possible control over circumstances, that he lets circumstances have the least possible control over him.

Goethe

God gave us the nuts, but he will not crack them.

Goethe

If life is considered a task, then life can always be endured.

Ebner-Eschenbach

Practical Wisdom

In the face of even the greatest loss we must instantly review what is left to us to do.

Goethe

What would life be without hope? A spark that flies from the embers and is extinguished, and just as you hear a gust in winter whistle for a while and then die out, so it would be with us. There would be no life were there not hope.

Hölderlin

Misfortune forms a man and obliges him to know himself.

Goethe

I have learned much in sickness that I could not have learned in other circumstances of my life.

Goethe

In extreme suffering certain protective mechanisms of the soul are also activated.

Freud

There remains one joy for us always. Genuine pain inspires. He who steps on his misery stands taller. And it is sublime that only in suffering do we truly feel the soul's freedom.

Hölderlin

Knowledge of Human Nature ·

Art of Living

Knowledge of Human Nature

He who knows himself will soon know all other people.

Lichtenberg

He who wants to be a judge of human nature should study people's excuses.

Hebbel

It is a sure sign of self-knowledge to find more fault in yourself than in others.

Hebbel

To judge a man correctly, one must observe him not in his behavior toward those to whom he is tied by interests of whatever kind, actively or passively. He is to be observed in the way he behaves toward those from whom he can never expect an advantage of either a material or psychic nature.

Schnitzler

We do not get to know people by their coming to us. We must go to them to find out what they are like.

Goethe

Practical Wisdom

To know what other people think about some matter that concerns us, we need only consider what we would think of them under the same circumstances. No one should be regarded as morally better in this respect than oneself, nor as more stupid.

Lichtenberg

Never does a man describe his own character more clearly than by his way of describing that of others.

Jean Paul

You recognize stupid and intelligent people by the former's revering what appeals to them and the latter's feeling about what they lack.

Grillparzer

The more stupid a person is, the more delight he takes in himself.

Nestroy

Through nothing do people reveal their character more than by what they laugh about.

Goethe

People judge nothing more hastily than people's characters. I have always found that the so-called bad fellows gain when you know them better and that the good fellows lose.

Lichtenberg

People do not think as differently about the events of life as they talk about them.

Lichtenberg

In the last analysis, everything boils down to how one evaluates himself.

Fontane

He only profits from praise who values criticism.

Heine

Art of Living

———•·•———

Losing an illusion makes you wiser than finding a truth.

Börne

To rue nothing is the beginning of all wisdom.

Börne

Get your mind accustomed to doubting and your heart to being conciliatory.

Lichtenberg

Doubt must be nothing more than vigilance, otherwise it can become dangerous.

Lichtenberg

Words are no more than words, and when they glide along so very lightly, be on your guard. Horses pulling a wagon with heavy freight canter at a slow pace.

Claudius

The surest way to cultivate and preserve a friendly relation is to communicate to each other what we are doing; for people are much more likely to agree in what they do than in what they think.

Goethe

If you have the good, you should not long for the better, thereby incurring all kinds of risks.

Fontane

Troubles are pills which it is better to swallow than to chew.

Lichtenberg

One should seek the company of only such people who call for the exercise of one's good behavior.

Feuchtersleben

To live light-heartedly but not recklessly, to be gay without being boisterous, to be courageous without being bold, to show trust and cheerful resignation without fatalism—this is the art of living.

Fontane

To dismiss the past, to leave the future to Providence—
either one means to fail to understand the true meaning of the present, which can be considered reality only
insofar as it knows how to preserve the past through a
sense of responsibility.

Schnitzler

No blessing is equal to the blessing of work. Only life-
long work entitles a man to say: I have lived.

Goethe

Every day one should at least hear one little song, read
one good poem, see one fine painting and—if at all
possible—speak a few sensible words.

Goethe

How little man needs, and how comforting it is, when
he realizes how much he needs that little!

Goethe

The Body Politic · Patriotism · Ideologies

The Body Politic · Patriotism · Ideologies

It is in the nature of politics that its direction is absolutely purposeful, that consequently ethical motives, however often they are pretended, cannot be considered at all. That in such an atmosphere absolute and enduring, spiritual or ethical values can never thrive—who would doubt that?

Schnitzler

The state must be concerned about order, health, and security. As soon as it arrogates to itself influence on questions of ethics, art, and philosophy, it not only makes a fool of itself but, because of its power, becomes a danger to ethics, art, and philosophy.

Schnitzler

"What use the prattle? All my life I have never bothered about politics!" "What use, my friend? It bothers about you every moment of your life!"

Schnitzler

It is the ultimate purpose of all culture to make what we call "politics" superfluous but science and art indispensable to mankind.

Schnitzler

Patriotism corrupts history.

Goethe

There is no patriotic art and no patriotic science. Like all that is sublime and good, both belong to the whole world. They can be fostered only by the free and unlimited interaction of all contemporaries, always paying due respect to the heritage of the past.

Goethe

Just now, admittedly, most peoples are still intent on developing, or rather exploiting, their sense of nationalism in order to achieve internal unity. But the sense of nationalism is only a means to an end, it will disappear again when the latter is attained and thus has no great future. The future belongs to world citizenship, which is bound to come to power sooner or later, and, when it does, forever.

Goethe

It is a curious thing with national hatred. You will always find it most marked and vehement at the lowest stage of culture. Yet, there is a stage at which it vanishes altogether, where one stands above nations, so to speak, sharing the joy or sorrow of neighboring people, as though they had been encountered by one's own.

Goethe

Nationalism is championed by all those who create and exploit human misery.

Heinrich Mann

And you politicians, grown gray in battle, are still mouthing the old concept of native land, without realizing at all that the people united under the same flag often differ more from one another than from their immediate neighbors—although these are called foreigners.

Heinrich Mann

The best patriot will always be he who has benefited his country most, not he who has loved it most fervently.

Schnitzler

I love my country not because it is my country but because I think it is beautiful. I have a feeling for my native land, but it is not patriotism.

Schnitzler

I do not identify with someone because he and I happen to belong to the same nation, profession, race, or family. Whom I wish to be related to, is solely my affair. I recognize no innate responsibility in this matter. I have fellow citizens in every nation, comrades in every profession, and brothers who have no inkling of my existence.

Schnitzler

Let us remain citizens of our age *in the flesh*, for there is no other way. But *in the spirit* it is the privilege and the duty of philosopher and poet to belong to no nation and to no age but to be, in the full sense of the term, a contemporary of all ages.

Schiller

I believe I am above suspicion of being a champion of communism. Nevertheless, I cannot but see something superstitious and childish in the terror the world feels for the word communism and on which fascism has fed for so long. It is the basic folly of our time.

Thomas Mann

Socialism means the dutiful resolve no longer to hide one's head in the sand of heavenly things but siding with those who want to give this earth meaning— human meaning.

Thomas Mann

On the other hand, we must not make the mistake of blaming capitalism for all social and political ailments and assume that the mere introduction of socialism will suffice to cure all social and political ills. The danger of such a belief lies in the fanatical intolerance into which socialism's adherents lapse so easily by making a kind of church out of a social institution and by branding as wicked evildoers all those who do not belong to it.

Einstein

My aversion to communism has really nothing in common with the fear of the millionaire who trembles for his money; no, what disquiets me is the secret dread of the artist and scholar who sees our whole modern civilization, the accomplishments of many centuries, threatened.

Heine

The world that will come after us, in which our children and our grandchildren will live and which slowly begins to unveil its contours, can hardly be imagined without communist features: that is, without the basic idea of communal rights of possession and enjoyment of the goods of the earth; without gradual leveling of class differences; without the right to work and the duty to work being shared by all.

Thomas Mann

Just as the new cannot be understood if one is not anchored in the traditional, love of the old must remain wrong and sterile to one who shuts himself off from the new, which by historical necessity has sprung from the old.

Thomas Mann

The proletariat should neither rule nor should it exist at all. It should struggle to overcome itself and not to encompass all of us in itself.

Heinrich Mann

I long for the supranational state. Nationhood is the shape of today's power; the nation state has lost all sense and meaning.

Heinrich Mann

Not pacifism—but world organization.

Rathenau

To be a patriot and to want to bring one's influence to bear on the humanities and sciences makes one a dirty fellow who ought to be thrown out. For in a realm concerned with what is purely and universally human, where truth, clarity, and beauty alone should hold sway, what can be more impertinent than to want to weigh the scales with a prejudice for the nation to which one's own precious person happens to belong, and on that account now to do violence to truth, now to be unjust to the great minds of other nations in order to extol the minor figures of one's own?

Schopenhauer

Freedom and Oppression · Equality

Force · War and Peace

Freedom and Oppression

There is no man who does not love freedom, but the just demands it for all, the unjust only for himself.

Börne

The concern of all for freedom is necessary, for it is the most precious good. It does not fall into your lap by itself nor is it maintained automatically. It can be preserved only where people are aware of it and feel responsible for it. For freedom is always on the defensive and therefore in danger. Where the danger is no longer felt, freedom is already almost lost.

Jaspers

Usually a man who possesses great power finds it his pleasure to oppress all around him by his omnipotence and to see the world on its knees before him. The aim of a truly great mind will be to have everybody at the same level with himself. He will appreciate his own dignity the most if everybody around him perceives his own dignity. He who lifts up a tree and holds it up is stronger than the one who strikes it down. He who can rule only at the expense of reason and human dignity will not even hold power for long. Where little men bow before the powerful, the powerful are never quite safe from the powerless. Man may give up his dignity, but he will never become a friend of the one who robbed him of it.

Seume

Lawless power is the most terrible weakness.

Herder

Nothing is so unworthy of man than the toleration of force, for force negates him. Whoever inflicts force upon us, denies us nothing less than our humanity. Whoever submits to it, casts away his humanity.

Schiller

Away with the new witch doctrine, away with the base fatalism which shouts to us: The strong should rule, and the weak should serve. A higher voice calls: The just should rule, and the free will obey.

Arndt

You *should*, because I want it, is nonsense. But that *you* shall because *I* shall is a correct conclusion and the basis of all law.

Seume

Unconditional obedience is unthinkable between rational people. If somebody can use me according to his whims, I do not owe him obedience. This follows from man's moral nature.

Seume

What shows the character of true freedom and its proper use most clearly, is its misuse.

Jaspers

Freedom and Oppression

Governments that suppress freedom of speech, because they find the truths thus spread to be troublesome, act like children who cover their eyes so that they are not seen.

Schiller

Freedom of thought is opposed, first, by governmental constraint. True, they say, the powers that be can take from us the freedom to speak or to write, but not the freedom to think. But how much and how well would we think, if we did not think in communion with others, to whom we communicate our thoughts as they do theirs to us? Hence we may well say that any external power that deprives man of his freedom to state his thoughts publicly also deprives him of the freedom of thought.

Kant

Which government is the best? That which teaches us to govern ourselves.

Goethe

For countries ruled by despots there is no salvation but in ruin.

Schiller

Drive out fear! Then there is hope that the good spirit will move in.

Seume

You can let a man have his freedom but you cannot give it to him.

Schiller

Happy slaves are the most bitter enemies of freedom.

Ebner-Eschenbach

The acme of slavery: you don't know that you are enslaved.

Stoessl

A nation that can be saved only by a single man deserves to be beaten. Where there is oppression within, it will soon also come from the outside.

Seume

The issue is not that the power be in this hand or that; power itself must be reduced in whosoever hand it be.

Börne

The elemental reaction against injustice and for justice has been lost—that reaction which alone in the long run safeguards man's only protection against a relapse into barbarism. For I am convinced that the passionate will for justice and truth has contributed more to the improvement of man's circumstances than the calculating political cunning which in the long run only creates universal distrust. Who will doubt that Moses was a better guide for mankind than Machiavelli?

Schweitzer

Freedom and Oppression

Truth and freedom belong together as do lying and violence. Only truth can unite the free world; it is lost without truth. Freedom and untruth cannot exist together. Only a free world can achieve peace. It will not fight lies by lies. Every lie is one step on the path to totalitarianism.

Jaspers

Never do we hear more talk of freedom than when one party wants to subjugate the other with nothing else the issue than that power, influence, and property pass from one hand to another. Freedom is the whispered password of stealthy conspirators, the clamorous battle cry of avowed revolutionaries, indeed, the slogan of despotism itself, as it leads its subjugated masses forward against the foe promising surcease from oppression for all time.

Goethe

The more decisively a political party comes to power, the more lamentably the idea dissipates under whose banner it achieved victory, and presenting themselves as legitimate heirs are those bastards of the idea: dogmas.

Schnitzler

A revolution will perhaps bring about a reduction of personal despotism and profit-greedy or tyrannical oppression, but never a genuine reform of people's mentality. New prejudices, just as the old ones, will lead the thoughtless masses by the nose.

Kant

Lawgivers or revolutionaries who promise equality and liberty at the same time are either utopian dreamers or charlatans.

Goethe

It is true, I could not be a friend of the French revolution, for its atrocities were too close to me and shocked me every hour of the day, while its beneficial consequences could not yet be seen at that time.

Goethe

What reduces the idea of terrorism completely *ad absurdum* is the fact that ultimately, of necessity, no matter with what hostility the most extreme factions may oppose one another in their political views, in the course of events they customarily join forces. The reason for this is simply that these factions have put the ideas of violence—ideas which inevitably unite them—above the specific ideas that they are presumed to stand for. Terrorism will certainly always gain a brutal superiority for a while, but never real victory—which in the long run can be achieved only through the mind. The superiority of physical strength is limited in time, because according to physiological laws it must, little by little, become exhausted, whereas the mind is regenerated again and again from within itself. And so, of necessity, the mind is victorious over violence—the mind gains victory through the word, and born of the mind, is immortal.

Schnitzler

I agree entirely with the monarchists on the principle of trying to preserve what is established and ward off revolutionary change, but not on their means. The fact is that they call stupidity and darkness to their aid, while I look to reason and light.

Goethe

It is difficult to reconcile yourself to the errors of the times: if you resist them, you stand alone; if you yield to them, you have neither honor nor joy.

Goethe

The world can be brought forward only by those who oppose it.

Goethe

I find more and more that it is well to be on the side of the minority, since it is always the more intelligent.

Goethe

Moralism always inclines to iconoclasm. The dominance of ideology easily leads to hostility to art and culture.

Thomas Mann

To think and to observe humanely means to think and observe apolitically.

Thomas Mann

The more corrupt an age, the greater the contempt for women. The more despotic the form of government, the more women will become maids of slaves.

Jean Paul

Experience has taught us that freedom without brotherhood leads to anarchy, and equality without brotherhood to tyranny.

Coudenhove-Kalergi

Those who preach hatred will not redeem you.
Ebner-Eschenbach

Freedom must be strong, it must believe in itself and in its right to defend itself. It must be a freedom with authority. It must not allow itself to be seduced through having doubts about its rights, it must know how to defend itself against the cunning that wants to misuse freedom in order to kill it.

Thomas Mann

How disastrous if people in good faith forego violence, because they believe in nonviolence! They will then be subdued the more completely by the violence that hides behind the veil of its fraudulent doctrine.

Jaspers

One must not wait until the fight for freedom is called high treason.

Kästner

Freedom is still more than ever the light and the soul of the Occident.

Thomas Mann

We had freedom of thought to the extent that we kept the thoughts to ourselves. For this was a kind of leash law for our thoughts. We were permitted to have them but we had to keep them on the leash. If you let them loose, they killed you. In a word, we had a multitude of freedoms but no trace of freedom.

Nestroy

Reaction is a spectre, but spectres are only for the timid.

Nestroy

Equality · Force

Freedom and equality, they contradict each other and can never come to an ideal union, because equality carries in itself the seeds of tyranny, and freedom anarchical disintegration. It is mankind's task today to find a new equilibrium between them and to allow them to form a new union, in which it cannot be denied that the greatest possible realization of justice, the dominating idea of the epoch, has become a matter of the world's conscience.

Thomas Mann

Equality neither exists nor is it desirable but to assume it is a humane gesture. It should be that courtesy of the heart which is not only *related* to love.

Thomas Mann

Equalization of people beyond equality of opportunity
is the greatest injustice.

Jaspers

People's innate inclinations and talents are different.
Attempting to eliminate those differences was the tyr-
anny of which Lykurgus, Philippe II, Robespierre, and
Louis XVI made themselves guilty.

Börne

Philosophers have interpreted the world differently;
the point is to change it.

Marx

There must be no tolerance of intolerance. There must
be no freedom to destroy freedom.

Jaspers

Tolerance must be no more than a passing sentiment;
it must lead to recognition. Tolerating means insult-
ing.

Goethe

Where the wishes and strength of a people's majority
are ripe for freedom, there is no need for conspiracy;
where they are not, conspiracy will not succeed. For
even if it succeeds in toppling the old tyranny, a new
one will replace it.

Börne

War and Peace

War is in truth a disease, in which the body juices that serve health and preservation are used to nourish something foreign that is at odds with the organism.

Goethe

They say he died the glorious death of a hero. Why do they never say he suffered the magnificent mutilation of a hero? They say he gave his life for his country. Why do they never say he has had both legs amputated for his country?

Schnitzler

Only when I meet someone blinded in combat who, even at the price of his sight, would not renounce having actively and passively participated in these great times, then and only then shall I believe it really was a great epoch.

Schnitzler

Time is a precious gift, given us that in it we become wiser, more mature. It is peace itself. War is nothing but the savage scorning of time, the breaking out of it in mindless impatience.

Thomas Mann

The military could easily live without war. They could do quite well with maneuvers. Only the diplomats need war urgently.

Schnitzler

Shortly after World War I, an old Austrian colonel, sitting in a Vienna coffee house, grumbled: What a wonderful army we had, the Deutschmeister, the Kaiserjäger, the Tyrolian marksmen, the dragoons, and the artillery, no better army in all the world. And what did they do with them? They sent them to war!

(A truth in the garb of a joke)

Anon.

War has never actually been waged for an idea, neither a national nor a religious one. Ideas are always used as a pretense—they are, so to speak, carried ahead as a banner, as the flags of the soul. Naturally, any phrase can be elevated to the status of an idea. This is one of the principal tasks of the politician—who in turn restores the balance by making a phrase of every idea.

Schnitzler

Every war is started under the emptiest pretenses, carried on for good reasons, and concluded by the most mendacious pretexts.

Schnitzler

Our modern wars make many unhappy while they last and none happy when they are over.

Goethe

World history is a conspiracy of diplomats against common sense.

Schnitzler

The terminology of war has been coined by diplomats, the military, and those in power. It should be revised by those who have come back from the war, by the widows, the orphans, the physicians, and the poets.

Schnitzler

He who believes a threatening war to be a certainty contributes to its coming. He who believes peace to be a certainty becomes unconcerned and, without wanting it, helps the drift toward war. Only he who sees the danger and does not for a moment forget it can act responsibly and do what is possible to banish the danger.

Jaspers

No sooner can there be happier times than when all peoples have realized that every war, even a victorious one, is a national catastrophe. Even the power of a ruler cannot bring about this conviction. It can come only out of better religious and ethical education of the peoples.

Kant

So long as war is considered a possibility at all—i.e., so long as there are professions based on the possibility of war, and even so long as there is just one person who can acquire wealth or increase it by means of war, and that person is one who has the power or the influence to bring about war—just so long will there be wars.

Here and nowhere else must one come to grips with the problem of world peace—not in the realm of religious or philosophical or ethical motives. These are totally irrelevant. Neither to reason nor to compassion nor to honor can we appeal with the slightest hope of success. It is exclusively a question of so reconstructing the world that no person, not even a single one, be it in the country of friend or foe, has the slightest chance to improve his personal fortunes through war. Impossible? So long as that is impossible the peace movement has not the faintest chance of success. Neither with profundities nor with sentimentalities will you touch the hearts either of the diplomats or those of the defense contractors.

Schnitzler

On the battlefields of Verdun war left a legacy. Daily the chorus of the dead says: Have a better memory!

Kästner

The war following the next one will be decided by nothing more than bow and arrow.

Einstein

Many feuilletonists claim that after this war humanity will somehow be cleansed and purified.

The reasons for this assumption are not clear: none of the wars thus far waged in the world has produced this result.

Political reaction is almost invariably the consequence of victorious wars; revolution, the consequence of lost ones. Both consequences are, as it were, conditions of exhaustion.

Schnitzler

Never is peace achieved by coexistence; only by cooperation can it be accomplished.

Jaspers

Peace cannot be preserved by force. It can only grow out of agreements.

Thomas Mann

The fateful question for the human species seems to me to be whether and to what extent their cultural development will succeed in mastering the disturbance of their communal life by the human instinct of aggression and self-destruction.

Freud

We must revolutionize our thinking, we must revolutionize our doing, and we must have the courage to revolutionize also relations among peoples. Clichés of yesterday don't do today and will be hopelessly outmoded tomorrow. An immense effort is indispensable. If we fail to establish a supernational organization now, one will be established later, but then upon the ruins of a large part of the presently existing world.

Einstein

Today's problem is not atomic energy but man's heart.

Einstein

Books · Writing

The Ancients · Poetry and Art

Music

Books · Writing

The world by itself does not educate a man fully. The reading of the best writers must be added.

Lessing

Every important book should be read twice. First, one understands things better in their context if one knows the end. Second, because at the time of another reading one is in a different mood or frame of mind from one's first reading, which makes for a different impression. It is as if you saw an object under different illumination.

Freud

What is not worth reading more than once, does not deserve to be read at all.

Weber

Of bad books you can never read too few, and of good ones never too many; bad books are intellectual poison, they corrupt the spirit. In order to read what is good, it is a precondition that one not read what is bad, for life is short, time and energy limited.

Schopenhauer

The sure sign of a good book is that you like it more
and more the older you become.

Lichtenberg

The more our acquaintance with good books in-
creases, the smaller becomes the circle of people whose
company we enjoy.

Feuerbach

On surface contemplation of a library one feels as if in
the presence of a vast capital yielding silently incalculable interest.

Goethe

A book is like a child, it needs its own gestation time.
Books hastily written within a few weeks arouse in
me a certain prejudice against the author. A proper
woman does not bring her child into the world before
nine months are up.

Heine

Many people read only so as not to have to think.

Lichtenberg

True readers are those who invent along with the
book, and beyond it. For no poet provides a ready-
made heaven. He merely sets up a Jacob's ladder on
this lovely earth. The mysterious letters remain forever
dead to the listless sluggard who lacks the spirit to

mount the airy golden rungs. He would do better to dig trenches and cut furrows than waste his time in useless reading.

Eichendorff

Lessing's confession that he had read almost too much for the health of his mind, shows how healthy his mind was.

Lichtenberg

Among the greatest discoveries the human mind has made in recent times may be counted the art of evaluating a book without having read it.

Kant

A book is a mirror; when a monkey looks in, no apostle can look out.

Lichtenberg

He writes in such a way that even an angel's mind stops dead.

Lichtenberg

All poets and writers infatuated with the superlative aim higher than they can reach.

Nietzsche

For me the greatest beauty always lay in the greatest clarity.

Lessing

What makes a prolific author is often not his great knowledge but rather the fortunate relation between his abilities and his taste, by which the latter always approves what the former have created.

Lichtenberg

Everywhere there are genteel poor, but not among writers.

Ebner-Eschenbach

He who occupies himself with books constantly and exclusively is half lost for practical life.

Seume

He swallowed a lot of wisdom, but it seemed as if all of it had gone down the wrong way.

Lichtenberg

More than gold, lead has changed the world. And more than lead in the gun has it been lead in the printing font.

Lichtenberg

Nine-tenths of today's literature serves no other purpose than that of cheating some ducats out of the public's pockets. To this end author, publisher, and reviewer have firmly conspired.

Schopenhauer

The Ancients

———•———

Studying the writers of antiquity is very properly called the study of the humanities. For through them the student becomes first and foremost humanized again, in that he enters a world free from all the caricatures of the Middle Ages and Romanticism. These later so deeply infiltrated the European mind that even now a man is born into a world still blemished by them and so must first rid himself of them before he can, above all, again become humanized.

Schopenhauer

Never mind studying contemporaries and those who strive with you. Study the great men of the past, whose works have maintained their value and stature for centuries. A truly gifted man will naturally so incline; and the desire to delve into the great precursors is the very mark of a higher endowment. Study Molière, study Shakespeare, but above all study the ancient Greeks, ever and always the Greeks.

Goethe

Of all peoples it was the Greeks who dreamed the dream of life most beautifully.

Goethe

May the study of Greek and Roman literature forever remain the basis of higher cultivation.

Goethe

The ancients are the only ones who never grow old.

Weber

The wind that blows from the graves of the ancients wafts a fragrance as if from a mound of roses.

Goethe

Poetry and Art

Art broadens life and affords the individual, with all his limitations, a chance of losing himself in what is outside him and beyond his reach; this is art's finest effect.

Lichtenberg

It is the highest task of every art to employ appearance to create the illusion of a higher reality. But it is a false endeavor to carry the realization of appearance to such a point as to leave nothing in the end but ordinary reality.

Goethe

Genuine art . . . does not have as its object a mere transitory game. Its serious purpose is not merely to transform the human being into a momentary dream of freedom but actually to make him free.

Schiller

Poetry and Art

All great art idealizes the world instead of imitating it. Great artists are seers: through objects they penetrate to the archetypes into the realm of ideas, to form them into works of art, and to give the world the mirrored splendor of those more perfect ideas.

Coudenhove-Kalergi

Art is spirit, and spirit does not at all have to feel obligated to society, to community. Art that "goes to the people," that meets the need of the multitude, of the little man, its own, will disintegrate.

Thomas Mann

The homeland of all morality is art. It gives direction and uniqueness, it enlivens man's wretched life through manifold interpretations, it provides variety for the moments of tension, and so lightens the burden on man's shoulders.

Stoessl

A fine work of art can and will have moral effects, but to demand moral goals of the artist means to ruin his craft.

Goethe

Poetry is mankind's mother tongue.

Herder

The poets all write as though they were sick and the whole world a hospital. They speak of the grief and sorrow of this world and of the joys of the hereafter;

and malcontent as they are, one and all, each incites the other to ever greater dissatisfaction. This is indeed misusing poetry, which is really meant to smooth over life's petty strife and make man content with the world and his own state.

Goethe

There never were generally valid laws on what art should be. The vulgar, the unabashed, the disgusting have, as far as I know, never been included in the concept that defined art, but at different times the concept of what is vulgar, shameless, repulsive has changed.

Kollwitz

A poetic truth, because it is true in the absolute, can never be congruent with reality.

Goethe

The famous saying art is for all, is totally wrong; on the contrary, art is for very few, and sometimes it seems to me that there are fewer and fewer. Only beefsteak, which can more easily be followed than a music score, makes an increasing impact.

Fontane

Art is man's conscience.

Hebbel

Mankind dreams in its poets.

Herder

Music

The touchstone of true poetry is that it has the ability as a secular gospel to liberate us from the weight of our earthly burdens by an inner serenity and an outward sense of well-being.

Goethe

Music

The inexpressible emotion in our hearts evoked by all music that summons up a very intimate, yet eternally remote paradise—this emotion reflects every stirring of our innermost selves, even though it is completely independent of reality and far from its pain.

Schopenhauer

Art's dignity is probably most clearly manifested in music, because it has no extraneous material. It is all form and substance; it elevates and ennobles everything it expresses.

Goethe

What is music? It stands between thought and appearance; as a dawning mediator it stands between spirit and matter; it is related to both and yet different from both; it is spirit, but spirit that needs a time measure; it is matter, but matter that can dispense with space.

Heine

Listening to music is to me like listening to a sonorous past or a sonorous future. There is something holy to music. It cannot picture anything but the good—differing from other arts.

Jean Paul

Music in the best sense has little need of novelty; indeed the older it is and the more one is accustomed to it, the more effective it is.

Goethe

Music is higher revelation than all wisdom and philosophy.

Beethoven

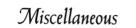

Miscellaneous

Miscellaneous

Thinking and doing, doing and thinking, that is the sum of all wisdom ... Like breathing in and out both must always alternate. He who makes it a rule to check thinking against doing, doing against thinking, cannot go astray, and if he should, he will soon find himself back on the right path.

Goethe

Man cannot dwell for long in a conscious state, or in consciousness. He must again take refuge in the unconscious, for that is where his life is rooted.

Goethe

The doctor sees man in all his weakness; the lawyer in all his wickedness; the theologian in all his stupidity.

Schopenhauer

He who has no friend, deserves none; a half truth. But that he who has no foe deserves no friend, might sooner be proved.

Seume

One's greatest pleasures are derived from the uneducated part of one's personality.

Goethe

Honor, objectively, is other people's opinion of our worth, and subjectively it is our fear of that opinion.

Schopenhauer

General concepts and great conceit are always poised to wreak dreadful havoc.

Goethe

If one is stupid, he is excused because it is not his fault. But if you offered the same excuse for one who is evil, you would be laughed at. Yet one is as congenital as the other. It is the "will" that is the real person, and reason merely the instrument of the will.

Schopenhauer

You only really know when you know little; with knowledge comes doubt.

Goethe

It is not consciousness that determines being, but being that determines consciousness.

Marx

The real social problem does not consist in the nourishing value of work but in its satisfying value.

Stoessl

Tolerance means: to excuse peoples' faults. Tact means: not to notice them.

Schnitzler

It often takes more courage to change one's opinion than to stick to it.

Lichtenberg

If thine own value you would relish
The world with worth you must embellish.

Goethe

The poorer a man's intellectual endowment is, the less puzzling does existence itself appear to him. On the contrary, everything, as it is and that is, will appear to him self-evident.

Schopenhauer

The more you love yourself, the more you are your own enemy.

Ebner-Eschenbach

Nothing can contribute more to peace of soul than having no opinion at all.

Lichtenberg

Native intelligence can replace culture at almost any level, but no amount of culture can replace native intelligence.

Schopenhauer

Every attempt at improving the world on the premise that mankind is capable of ethical development or even that it is originally good, is doomed to failure. The notion of man's original goodness is thoroughly sentimental, therefore sterile, if not altogether dangerous; and still more absurd is the idea that people who believe in mankind are by this very belief of a nobler character than those who believe not at all in mankind but only, from case to case, in man.

Schnitzler

I cannot say indeed whether conditions will improve if they change. But this much I can say—that they must change, if they are to improve.

Lichtenberg

It is true in general, the sages of all times always said the same thing, and the fools, that is, the vast majority in every age have always done the same thing, that is, the opposite. And thus it will always be.

Schopenhauer

Death accompanies us at every step and enables us to use those moments when life smiles at us to feel more deeply the sweetness of life. Nay, the more certain the end, the more tempting the minute, the more urgent the reminder: Seize the day!

Fontane

We are far more present in others than in what we call our selves. It is the whole meaning of higher life to get out of our selves and to achieve a transfigured personality in others. If one thinks this through fully, death loses most of its horror, even if one puts aside the hope for continuation of one's personal life.

Immermann

Biographical Notes

———————◆◆◆———————

Arndt, Ernst Moritz (1769–1860). Poet and historian, he taught history at the University of Bonn and was an ardent nationalist and opponent of Napoleon. He was forced to flee to Sweden and Russia after the publication of his book *Geist der Zeit* [Spirit of the Times]. His patriotic verse helped to influence German feelings against Napoleon.

Beethoven, Ludwig van (1770–1827). Born in Bonn, he lived in Vienna from 1772 until his death. He earned early renown as a pianist, but his increasing deafness made a performing career impossible. The great works of his last years were composed in total deafness. Beethoven developed and enlarged the classical forms, thereby paving the way for the large-scale symphonic works of the 19th century. But beyond the musical realm he has come to be considered a prophet of the eternal ideas of mankind.

Börne, Ludwig (1786–1837). Writer of the group "Junges Deutschland" and a journalist, he was a radical protagonist for intellectual and political freedom. From 1830 on he lived in Paris, where he wrote his famous "Letters from Paris," which were largely passionate attacks on conditions in Germany. They are important as documents of the time. Börne was a masterful stylist and aphorist.

Biographical Notes

Brentano, Clemens (1778–1842). One of the great lyric poets of late romanticism, he also created folksongs and fairy tales of enduring beauty.

Busch, Wilhelm (1832–1908). Cartoonist, painter, and poet, he was the creator of the comic strip. A melancholy humorist, he is one of the most popular and most widely quoted German writers.

Claudius, Matthias (1740–1815). A great poet and a child-like soul, he put in naïve but touching verse the voices of his own devout heart. Founder of the newspaper *Der Wandsbecker Bote* (The Wandsbeck Messenger), he frequently wrote for it in the form of letters to his friends (and his son), aiming to serve the moral, Christian education of his community.

Coudenhove-Kalergi, Richard Graf (1894–1972). Historian and statesman, he achieved international renown with the publication in 1923 of his *Paneuropa*, in which he championed the confederation of European countries. He taught history at the New School for Social Research, New York, after World War II.

Ebner-Eschenbach, Marie von (1830–1916). One of the most important Austrian novelists, she is famous for her *Village and Castle Stories*, in which she depicted the life and customs of her native region with great empathy for the underprivileged and a deep feeling of responsibility for their well-being, although from an aristocratic, paternalistic viewpoint. Her writings are characterized by subtle psychological insights, knowledge of human nature, and an all-pervading humanity.

Eichendorff, Joseph von (1788–1857). The work of this last great representative of the Romantic period shows the unpretentious popular appeal of Romanticism in its purest crystallization. His narrative, and still more his poetic work, have remained a living treasure to German readers. Musical settings for many of his poems have achieved world-wide popularity.

Einstein, Albert (1879–1955). Theoretical physicist internationally famous for the formulation of the theory of relativity and for his contributions to the development of the quantum theory. Received the Nobel Prize in 1921. In 1939 he wrote President Roosevelt stressing the urgency of investigating the possible use of atomic energy in bombs, but, as an active pacifist, warned against their use.

Feuchtersleben, Ernst von (1806–1849). Physician, psychotherapist, and university professor, he was also a lyric poet and popular-philosophical writer. His *Dialetik der Seele* (Dialectic of the Soul), in which he taught physical health through the power of the will and the mind, was one of the most successful books of the century.

Feuerbach, Ludwig (1804–1872). Having begun his career as a believing theologian, he became the protagonist of militant atheism. His book *The Essence of Religion* was the arsenal and centerpiece of support for antireligious thought. He saw in religion only a dream of the human mind in the enrapturing light of wishful imagination. For religion makes God become man and then makes this God, who has human form, human feelings, and human thought, the object of worship. God is thus in reality merely the projected essence of man. Feuerbach's work has had an enormous influence not only on Marxists but also on many who were not communists, such as Nietzsche, Huxley, Freud, and John Dewey.

Fontane, Theodor (1819–1898). Journalist and narrative writer, he lived in England for many years as a foreign correspondent for German newspapers. An outstanding exponent of Realism, Fontane became famous for his poetry, particularly his ballads. He turned to writing novels in his sixties, first in the historical genre, but his real métier was novels dealing with love and marriage problems, with

the concept of honor, and the conflicts of a society domi-
nated by rigid class barriers. *Effi Briest* is his most famous
novel for English readers. His work is marked by skepti-
cal resignation, dry humor, and an understanding of human
weakness. Fontane is at his best in depicting the milieu and
in creating brilliant dialogues.

Freud, Sigmund (1856–1939). World-famous as the founder
of psychoanalysis, he has had an incalculable influence on
psychotherapy, anthropology, literature, and art. Although
his theories have not been universally accepted, he is considered one of mankind's great teachers and emancipators.

Goethe, Johann Wolfgang von (1749–1832). The greatest
poet of the German nation and the last great universal
genius the West produced, "who won the whole world as a
poet and sage, as a lover of life, as a hero of peace, as one
blessed by nature and intellect, as the idol of mankind"
(Thomas Mann). Goethe had immense influence on European literature and the intellectual history of modern times.
Unsurpassed as a lyric poet, he created in the drama and in
epic novels, timeless representatives of true humanity (*Iphi-
genia, Torquato Tasso, Hermann and Dorothea, Wilhelm
Meister's Apprenticeship*). His extensive autobiographical
writings, his letters, and recorded conversations are filled
with observations on the central problem of what the Ger-
mans call *Bildung*, the conscious, planned forming of character and spirit. His main work, *Faust*, and his two *Wilhelm
Meister* novels are built entirely around the question of the
ethical growth of the leading characters. In "The Pedagogi-
cal Province," a chapter in *Wilhelm Meister's Apprenticeship*, he represented idealized humanity as the only possible
basis of the good society built around concern for the vital
interests of one's fellows.

Görres, Joseph (1776–1848). One of Germany's greatest
prose writers, he founded his newspaper *Der Rheinische
Merkur* (1814–1860) and with it established the influence of
political journalism. First in sympathy with the French

Revolution, he later turned against it and called upon his fellow countrymen to rise against Napoleon. After Napoleon's downfall he attacked the German dynastic reaction and had to flee to Switzerland.

Grillparzer, Franz (1791–1872). Founding father of modern Austrian literature and his country's foremost dramatist, he carried on the tradition of Goethe and Schiller, adding formal elements of Romanticism, the Spanish-Catholic baroque theater, and the Vienna folk stage. Also a gifted narrative writer and literary critic, he wrote biting epigrams of sarcastic wit.

Hebbel, Christian Friedrich (1813–1863). Dramatist, narrative writer, author of profound diaries, poet, and critic. His work, permeated by a deeply tragic world view, ranges from idealism to a pessimistic psychological realism.

Heine, Heinrich (1797–1856). The greatest German lyric poet in the period between Romanticism and Realism, he combines melancholy, *Weltschmerz,* and sentimentality with witty irony. Heine created folksong-like love poems, masterful ballads, and political writings of merciless satire. He also originated the modern *feuilleton,* or journalistic essay.

Herder, Johann Gottfried (1744–1803). Poet, critic, and founder of the German philosophy of history, he made contributions to philology, comparative religion, and mythology. He was a most potent stimulus to German intellectual history, and his influence on his contemporaries reached far beyond his own country. Herder interpreted creatively the language, literature, and culture of a people by examining its historical roots as they were conditioned by character, climate, and landscape. His greatness is not to be found within the covers of a single work, but his surpassing importance for Goethe and Schiller and their contemporaries (the German classics) and also for Romanticism lies in his extraordinary empathy with foreign literature, his openness to the specifically national in all its manifestations, and in his feel for what has evolved organically. Herder compiled a trailblazing anthology of foreign folksongs. He saw in poetry "the mother tongue of mankind."

Hölderlin, Friedrich (1770–1843). One of Germany's greatest poets, he produced highly subjective poetry of a lofty style modeled on the classic Greek. Hölderlin's verse represents a link between the classic and romantic schools. His writing career ended with the onset of insanity at age 36.

Humboldt, Wilhelm von (1767–1835). A universal scholar, philologist, linguistic philosopher, and theoretician of German idealism and of a cosmopolitan humanism, he was a friend of Schiller, Goethe, and the Schlegels. Head of the Prussian education system and founder of Berlin University, he advocated restricting the rights of the state over the individual.

Immermann, Karl (Lebrecht) (1796–1840). Author of *Der Oberhof*, the earliest German novel of authentic realism.

Jaspers, Karl (1883–1969). He taught pyschology (1916), then philosophy (1921) at the University of Heidelberg and from 1948 on at the University of Basel. He developed a system of a humanistically oriented, highly individualistic philosophy, associated with existentialism as developed by Heidegger. In the dark age of National Socialism he represented "the other Germany," the *humanitas* of Germany.

Jean Paul [Johann Paul Friedrich Richter] (1763–1825). An important narrative writer of German Idealism with a highly subjective, often flowery style, he favored psychological penetration at the expense of plot in his stories. His inexhaustible, yarn-spinning imagination has a tendency toward the grotesque-comic and the lovingly drawn presentation of scurrilous characters.

Jung, Carl Gustav (1875–1961). Swiss psychiatrist and psychotherapist, he founded the school of analytical psychology and became editor of the *Jahrbuch für psychoanalytische und psychopathologische Forschungen* (Annual of Psychoanalytical and Psychopathological Research). At first he was in harmony with Freud's ideas, but important differences between the two men led to a formal break between them. Jung conceived of the libido as a primal, nonsexual energy and postulated two forms of the unconscious—the individual, made up of the repressed events of a person's life, and the collective, formed of the inherited tendencies of the race. His approach was mystical and religious in contrast to that of Freud.

Kant, Immanuel (1724–1804). Foremost German philosopher, whose incalculable influence on philosophical thought has been greater that that of any other philosopher after him.

Kästner, Erich (1899–1975). Novelist, poet, and writer of children's books translated into many languages, he was an ironic critic of his time, a moralist who attacked with flashing wit the inertia of heart and mind in his contemporaries. He also wrote radio plays and sketches for political cabarets.

Keller, Gottfried (1819–1890). Both as a narrative writer and a lyric poet he is universally regarded as one of the most beloved and original minds in German letters. He immortalized his pictures of the life he knew by balancing clear-eyed realism with sprightly imagination and a keen sense of humor. The Swiss writer's most famous novella is probably *A Village Romeo and Juliet*.

Kollwitz, Käthe (1867–1945). Painter, lithographer, and etcher, an ardent pacifist and socialist, she is best known for her lithographs of poor people, testimony to a deeply felt compassion. The advent of the Nazi party ended her public career. She is also noted as the author of a beautiful diary.

Lessing, Gotthold Ephraim (1729–1781). Dramatist, trailblazing critic, and theoretician of literature, art, and the theater, he was among the strongest voices for humanism in German literature and so cleared the way for the German classics. He was the creator of the German middle-class tragedy and is perhaps best known as author of *Nathan the Wise*, the drama of enlightened tolerance still frequently produced today. Lessing was a man of intellectual independence and incorruptible veracity, whose ethos exerted an indelible impact on German literature. He favored Shakespeare and opposed French classicism as falsifying the dramaturgical principles of Aristotle's *Poetics* and the ancient tragedians. He also wrote epigrams of biting wit and fables.

Lichtenberg, Georg Christoph (1742–1799). Professor of natural sciences, in particular experimental physics, he was the great satirist of the German enlightenment and master of the aphorism, attacking mysticism, superstition, and religious intolerance. He was also an influential art critic through his interpretation of Hogarth's engravings.

Ludwig, Otto (1813–1865). A talented novelist and dramatist whose fame rests largely upon two tales, *Die Heiterethei* [the title is the name of the main female character] and *Zwischen Himmel und Erde (Between Heaven and Earth).*

Mann, Heinrich (1871–1950). Novelist, essayist, and dramatist, politically engaged in most of his novels and novellas, he was a passionate social critic of the declining bourgeoisie. He fought nationalsm and militarism, and championed a democratic, humanistic socialism.

Mann, Thomas (1875–1955). The master German narrative writer, he expanded the scope of the traditional novel in many ways. Out of an alert interest in all currents of his time and as a cultural critic and educator advocating democracy and humanism, he wrote numerous important essays of a literary, political, and philosophical nature. He was awarded the Nobel Prize for Literature in 1929.

Biographical Notes

Marx, Karl (1818–1883). Social philosopher and chief theorist of scientific socialism, and its radical leader, he published in 1848, together with Friedrich Engels, the famous *Communist Manifesto* which set forth the basic formulation of Marxism. He went into exile in London, where he remained until his death. There he founded the International Workingmen's Association and wrote the monumental *Das Kapital*, in which he repudiated all existing social theories either as utopian or unsocialistic. This work has had a wider impact on the development of society than any other social or nonreligious document, despite the fact that many of Marx's basic predictions have not materialized or have been found to be wrong.

Mozart, Wolfgang Amadeus (1756–1791). Born in Salzburg, trained in music at an early age by his father, he was a child prodigy under the court of Maria Theresa and performed at the principal aristocratic households of Central Europe, as well as in Paris and London. In 1771 he resigned from the service of the Archbishop of Salzburg and moved to Vienna. His friendship with Haydn was a great influence on Mozart's work, particularly his string quartets. Haydn in turn considered him the greatest living composer. Mozart excelled in all musical forms, but perhaps his greatest achievement is his operatic work.

Nestroy, Johann Nepomuk (1801–1882). He is the most representative figure of the Viennese folk theater and the greatest German satiric playwright. An actor, he wrote his comedies largely for want of existing suitable plays, proving himself a superb comedian. Endowed with a sharp eye for the weaknesses and symptoms of disintegration in the Austrian society of his day, he was an unfailing judge of human nature. His seemingly unpretentious slapstick comedies of earthy comicality concealed profound philosophical insights. As described by Egon Friedell, he was "a Socratic dialectician, a Kant-like analytical mind of utmost subtlety and pungency, pitilessly undermining life-falsifying illusions and pathos, with a truly Shakespearean intellect, wit, and humor that contorted and disarranged the measurement of all human things only to shine forth in their true dimensions." This laughing and deeply thoughtful playwright had a mind equally liberal and conservative, one of extraordinary independence. His unusual mastery of language, his verbal pyrotechnics pose difficult translation problems. So far only three of his some eighty comedies have appeared in English. An untapped gold mine remains. *Hello, Dolly!* was based on *The Matchmaker* by Thornton Wilder, a Nestroy admirer who derived its plot from Nestroy's *Einen Jux will er sich machen* (He wants to enjoy a prank).

Nietzsche, Friedrich Wilhelm (1844–1900). Philosopher, essayist, aphorist, and poet, professor of classical philology in Basel (1869), a cultural critic of world-wide influence on thinkers and writers of the 20th century. Descended from an old family of Protestant preachers, Nietzsche opposed idealistic philosophy through analysis of the sham values of a "slave morality" such as asceticism, compassion, Christianity, and socialism. Against these he proposed a vitalistic philosophy based on the will to power and an aristocratic master morality *(Herrenmoral)*. His heroic nihilism and atheism strove to give meaning to the senselessness of life by a "transvaluation of values." Insanity overtook him in 1889, and he remained mentally deranged until his death.

Planck, Max (1889–1928). Professor of physics at the University of Berlin, he developed, on the basis of research in thermodynamics, his revolutionary quantum theory. He received the Nobel Prize in Physics in 1918.

Popper-Lynkeus, Josef (1838–1921). Technical inventor and social reformer, he was the first to propose electrical power transmission. He championed the idea of replacing military service by the introduction of compulsory national food production service *(Nährarmee)*, an idea still worthy of consideration today.

Biographical Notes

Rathenau, Walter (1867–1922). German industrialist, social theorist, and statesman, he directed the distribution of raw materials in World War I, became Minister of Reconstruction in 1921 and Foreign Minister in 1922. He was assassinated by nationalist and anti-Semitic fanatics, who opposed his sincere attempts to fulfill reparation obligations.

Schiller, Friedrich (1759–1805). One of the world's greatest dramatists and a brilliant representative of German idealism. A lyric poet of widest popularity, he also excelled as a narrative and historical writer. His philosophical-aesthetical writings also are of enduring value. Attaining inner freedom was the basic concern and goal of his life. In it the creative power of the mind triumphs over fate and the world of earthly reality.

Schnitzler, Arthur (1862–1931). Novelist, dramatist, short-story writer, and essayist, he portrayed in masterful fashion the Vienna society of the turn of the century. A perceptive judge of human nature, he was trained as a physician and was deeply interested in psychology. In his work he anticipated many of Freud's theories. Freud himself referred to his fellow Viennese as his "Doppelgänger." Schnitzler's social and psychological insights were decades ahead of his time. His reflections, as contained in *Buch der Betrachtung* (Book of Contemplation), *The Mind in Words and Actions,* and *Some Day Peace Will Return* (the latter two available in English translation, Ungar, 1972), are contributions to philosophy in its fundamental sense, the study of man's psychic nature.

Schopenhauer, Arthur (1788–1860). Perhaps no philosopher ever looked at the world, and at human nature, more penetratingly than he. Convinced of the illusional character of the world, he based his philosophy on Kantian idealism. He argued that the true reality is a blind impelling force, the will to live often working below the level of consciousness,

147

and that our world is one of unsatisfied wants and pain. Although Schopenhauer recognized the feebleness of the intellect against the powerful sway of instinct, he believed that renunciation of desires, negation of the will can lead to the redemption from the animalistic aspects of man's nature. And so let him find at least temporary escape. The ethical side of his philosophy is based on sympathy, where the moral will, feeling another's hurt as his own, makes an effort to relieve the pain. Schopenhauer's profound insight into the tragic and irrational nature of man made him the precursor of the most advanced of modern thinkers.

Schweitzer, Albert (1875–1965). Philosopher, theologian, physician, and musician, he went in 1913 to Labarené, in what is now Gabon, then French Equatorial Africa, to establish a hospital, which he supervised to the end of his life. He is honored in many countries for his work as a scientist and humanitarian.

Seume, Johann Gottfried (1763–1810). Author of memoirs, descriptions of his travels in Russia, Finland, Sweden, and Italy, and a poet. His life was full of adventures, most of which brought him unhappiness. Seized by recruiters, he was sold to England by the landgrave of Hesse, Frederick II, was forced into the English army to fight as a Hessian recruit, and shipped to the American colonies. Upon his return to England in 1783, he deserted. Arrested and ultimately convicted, he was finally released after two unsuccessful jailbreaks, but he had to pay for his release by years of work. His autobiography and travel descriptions are of great cultural and historical interest.

Speidel, Ludwig (1830–1906). Witty yet profound observer and critic of the literary life of Vienna, and of its art and music. A model stylist, he was feuilletonist of *Neue Freie Presse;* Austria's leading newspaper.

Stoessl, Otto (1875–1936). Austrian novelist, poet, essayist, critic, and dramatist he carried on the tradition of the past masters of poetic realism, Keller, C. F. Meyer, and Stifter, in a truly noble way. What gives his novellas their vigor and conviction, beyond all aesthetic merits, is their profound humanity.

Weber, Karl Julius (1767–1832). Political writer, whose work reveals a scornful skepticism, reflecting the influence of the French encyclopedists. His satirical, humorous writings were widely read.

Copyright Acknowledgments

The editor and the publishers are grateful for the cooperation of those individuals and publishers who granted permission for the use of their copyrighted material. Every effort has been made to trace and acknowledge properly all copyright owners. If any acknowledgment has been inadvertently omitted, the publishers will be pleased to make the necessary correction in the next printing.

George Allen & Unwin Ltd. Selections by Albert Schweitzer were translated for this volume by permission of the publishers of the English edition of *Christianity and the Religions of the World*.

Atrium Verlag. For selections form *Kurz und Bündig* by Erich Kaestner.

Adams and Charles Black Ltd. Selections by Albert Schweitzer were translated for this volume by permission of the publishers of the English edition of *The Philosophy of Civilization*, Part I: *The Decay and the Restoration of Civilization*.

Estate of Albert Einstein, Otto Nathan, Trustee. For selections from *Out of My Later Years* by Albert Einstein, 1970, by permission of the Estate of Albert Einstein.

S. Fischer Verlag. For selections from *Gesammelte Werks: Aphorismen und Betrachtungen* by Arthur Schnitzler, © S. Fischer Verlag GmbH, Frankfurt am Main, 1967.

Eric Glass. For selections from *Gesammelte Werke: Aphorismen und Betrachtungen* by Arthur Schnitzler.

The Hogarth Press Ltd. For selections from "Civilization and Its Discontents" in *The Standard Edition of the Complete Works of Sigmund Freud*, Volume XXI.

Alfred A. Knopf, Inc. For selections from *Confessions of Felix Krull, Confidence Man* by Thomas Mann, translated by

Copyright Acknowledgments